I Remember

POEMS AND PICTURES OF HERITAGE

COMPILED BY LEE BENNETT HOPKINS

POEMS BY

Kwame Alexander • Jorge Tetl Argueta • Joseph Bruchac • Nick Bruel
Margarita Engle • Douglas Florian • Guadalupe García McCall
Marilyn Nelson • G. Neri • Naomi Shihab Nye • Cynthia Leitich Smith
Carole Boston Weatherford • Janet S. Wong • Jane Yolen

PICTURES BY

Paula Barragán • Sawsan Chalabi • R. Gregory Christie • Julie Downing
David Kanietakeron Fadden • Insoo Kim • Rafael López • Janine Macbeth
Juliet Menéndez • Daniel Minter • Sean Qualls • Charlotte Riley-Webb
Jeanne Rorex Bridges • Simone Shin • Neil Waldman • Michele Wood

LEE & LOW BOOKS INC. NEW YORK

"Memories are such a large part of my creative process. Remembering feelings, places, and faces helps me to connect emotionally with whatever my subject is. I believe many artists do the same to some degree, and for me, this is what makes a work of art unique. Memory is a subjective filter and an intimate one that has the power to pull us into its realm and change the way we see."

—Sean Qualls, jacket artist

Art direction and design by Christy Hale
Production by The Kids at Our House
The text is set in ITC Century
The illustrations are rendered in various media
Manufactured in Malaysia by Tien Wah Press
10 9 8 7 6 5 4 3 2 1
First Edition

Library of Congress Cataloging-in-Publication Data
Names: Hopkins, Lee Bennett, compiler. | Alexander, Kwame, author. | Barragán, Paula, 1963- illustrator.
Title: I remember : poems and pictures of heritage / compiled by Lee Bennett Hopkins ; poems by Kwame Alexander [and thirteen others] ; pictures by Paula Barragán [and fifteen others].
Description: First edition. | New York : Lee & Low Books Inc., [2019] |
Summary: A collection of works by poets and illustrators of diverse backgrounds sharing memorable childhood and family experiences and reflecting on their different heritages, traditions, and beliefs.
Identifiers: LCCN 2019013101 | ISBN 9781620143117 (hardcover : alk. paper)
Subjects: LCSH: Families—Juvenile poetry. | Culture—Juvenile poetry. | Identity (Psychology)—Juvenile poetry. | Memory—Juvenile poetry. | Families—Pictorial works. | Culture—Pictorial works. | Identity (Psychology)—Pictorial works. | Memory—Pictorial works. | Children's poetry, American. | CYAC: Family life— Poetry. | Culture—Poetry. | Identity—Poetry. | Memory—Poetry. | American poetry.
Classification: LCC PS595.F34 I14 2019 | DDC 811/.608—dc23
LC record available at https://lccn.loc.gov/2019013101

To

Phyllis and Arthur Rieser
for your compassion, kindness,
and tender-heartedness

—L.B.H.

ACKNOWLEDGMENTS

Thanks are due to the following for use of the poems in this collection: Curtis Brown, Ltd. for "Amazing Auntie Anne" by Cynthia Leitich Smith. Copyright © 2019 by Cynthia Leitich Smith. "Calling Home" by Jane Yolen. Copyright © 2019 by Jane Yolen. Both used by permission of Curtis Brown, Ltd. Dunham Literary, Inc. for "Pick One" by Nick Bruel. Copyright © 2019 by Nick Bruel. Published by arrangement with Dunham Literary, Inc. as agent for the author. All other poems are used by permission of the respective poets, who control all rights; all copyright © 2019: Kwame Alexander for "Here's What I Remember"; Jorge Tetl Argueta for "Tepechapa River"; Joseph Bruchac for "Rez Road"; Margarita Engle for "La visita"; Douglas Florian for "Grandpa"; Guadalupe García McCall for "My Quinceañera"; Marilyn Nelson for "Route 66"; G. Neri for "Gumbo Nation"; Naomi Shihab Nye for "Far, Far Away (for Palestine)"; Carole Boston Weatherford for "What My Kinfolk Made"; Janet S. Wong for "Mother's Day" and "Speak Up."

Thanks are also due to the following for the illustrations in this collection; all copyright © 2019 by the individual artists: Paula Barragán, for the image accompanying "La visita"; Sawsan Chalabi for the image accompanying "Far, Far Away (for Palestine)"; R. Gregory Christie, for the image accompanying "Route 66"; Julie Downing, for the image accompanying "Calling Home"; David Kanietakeron Fadden, for the image accompanying "Rez Road"; Insoo Kim, for the image accompanying "Speak Up"; Rafael López, for the image accompanying "Tepechapa River"; Janine Macbeth, for the image accompanying "Pick One"; Juliet Menéndez, for the image accompanying "My Quinceañera"; Daniel Minter, for the image accompanying "What My Kinfolk Made"; Sean Qualls, for the jacket artwork; Charlotte Riley-Webb, for the image accompanying "Gumbo Nation"; Jeanne Rorex Bridges, for the image accompanying "Amazing Auntie Anne"; Simone Shin, for the image accompanying "Mother's Day"; Neil Waldman, for the image accompanying "Grandpa"; Michele Wood, for the image accompanying "Here's What I Remember."

Jello is a generic term based on Jell-O®, a registered trademark of Kraft Foods for varieties of sweetened and flavored gelatin and pudding.

Space Mountain® is a registered trademark of Walt Disney Productions Corporation for an amusement park ride.

Spam® is a registered trademark of Hormel Foods Corp. for a canned meat product.

Heritage makes us who we are. It is an essential, important part of us—our inherited traditions, beliefs, values, and achievements, and how we identify ourselves. Heritage also conjures up remembrances of family, events, travels, songs, celebrations, goals, and challenges. It is our past, our today, and our foundation to build on for the future.

The poems and pictures in this collection reflect a diversity of heartfelt voices who portray their yesterdays, singing out about where they came from and where they are, reflecting, recalling, and reliving memories to remind us all of their proud heritage.

Read.

       Look.

            Listen.

                  Hear.

                       See.

—Lee Bennett Hopkins

SIMONE SHIN

"Art to me is when you gather your past, present, and future and somehow express them as one; when you allow your memories, your current condition, and your hopes and dreams to vibrate together in harmony."

JANET S. WONG

"Poetry shows you what you are inside, what is on your mind or in your heart when you might not even know it."

Mother's Day

Mother's Day morning
and I have no present.
No money.
I walk outside.

Kicking the dirt,
my toes hit a rock.
A smooth speckled oval,
it could be a gargoyle egg.
Or a paperweight.
Stuck in a box,
wrapped in the gold paper
Mother saved from Christmas,
the old tape peeled off,
it looks like a good gift.

She shakes the box, smiling,
while I stare at her hands
untying the ribbon,
tearing the paper,
lifting the lid.
She holds the rock with flat fingers,
like some rotten egg.

Mother walks into the kitchen,
puzzling. She puts a clove of garlic
on her thick round cutting board
and brings the rock down hard.

"A garlic rock," she says,
pulling chunks of garlic
from the broken skin.
"Just what I needed."

Speak Up

You're Korean, aren't you?

                    Yes.

Why don't you speak
Korean?

                    Just don't, I guess.

Say something Korean.

                    I don't speak it.
                    I can't.

C'mon. Say something.

                    Halmoni. Grandmother.
                    Haraboji. Grandfather.
                    Imo. Aunt.

Say some other stuff.
Sounds funny.
Sounds strange.

                    Hey, let's listen to you
                    for a change.

Listen to me?

                    Say some foreign words.

But I'm American,
can't you see?

                    Your family came from
                    somewhere else.
                    Sometime.

But I was born here.

                    So was I.

Halmoni (HAL-mo-nee): Grandmother
Haraboji (HAH-rah-bo-jee): Grandfather
Imo (EE-moh): Aunt

INSOO KIM

"I've always been fascinated by illustration and animation because of the possibilities to create characters and worlds that exist in the realm of imagination and to share stories that can reach beyond the boundaries and limitations of the material world."

MICHELE WOOD

"I am the Artist you have come to know, dearest all. I am but a whisper. I am but a mere member of the Women of Faith. Faith is a mustard seed that grows with my painting gift from above."

KWAME ALEXANDER

"The power of poetry is that you can take emotionally heavy moments in your life and distill them into palatable, digestible words, lines, and phrases allowing us to deal, to cope with the world. I believe in the power of poetry to change the world."

Here's What I Remember

one hundred degree Sundays riding backseat in Dad's
caramel-colored Dodge Dart . . . after church, sweat
clinging like static; our heads out the window trying to
catch a breeze . . . on the way to High's Ice Cream Store—
paradise . . . i remember meat loaf . . . the way the butter in
Granny's rolls disappeared like snow on fingertips . . . the
way i disappeared when Granny's switch appeared . . .
the stuff i found in Granddaddy's attic . . . the money, the
letters to Granny, the WWII medals . . . summertime
reunions with cousins unseen since last summer, barbecue
for miles, aunts laughing at uncles singing a lot, and
dancing even more . . . dominoes and bid whist . . . good
times . . . the time we sat, steel-like in fear for two hours
in an Orlando hotel because my father couldn't find his
hat, and Space Mountain summoning us like a siren . . .
the names i called my sisters. bad . . . the looks they gave
me. worse . . . finding joy in traveling . . . never minding
moving . . . New York, North Carolina, Virginia . . . all in
the same year . . . counting cars, logging license plates,
travel games . . . winning the spelling bee. my father
smiling . . . relatives i never met (and the ones i wish i
hadn't) showing up for dinner . . . family meetings. which
were more like lectures with no Q&A. trials with no jury . . .
and seven days during Kwanzaa in December . . . my
mother cooking, my father trying (who ever heard of
macaroni and cheese and mustard?) . . . grocery store
checkout line quizzes (*if i have a coupon for $.50 off
and today is double coupon day and orange juice is
on sale, 2 for $3, then what is the cost including tax*)
with no reward for correct, and plenty of consequences
for incorrect . . . loved ones who passed. Nana. Uncle

Richard. Granddaddy. Ovie. Granny. Aunt Dorothy.
Granddaddy again . . . funerals. meeting new folks and
missing old ones . . . children playing, loving, smiling,
planning, crying, dreaming, laughing, and leaping forever
forward into their futures. i remember regularly sitting
in the living room fingering through the countless
memorabilia that my mother kept: scrapbooks, yearbooks,
old report cards, portraits, love letters, wedding photos.
i remember looking for . . . me. and always being proud
of what i found.

bid whist (bid wist): card game for two teams of two players each
Kwanzaa (KWAHN-zuh): celebration of family, community, and culture
    observed from December 26 to January 1 by African Americans and
    the world African community

MARGARITA ENGLE

*"Poetry is a bridge—between my own thoughts and feelings,
between separate individuals, and between cultures."*

La visita

When Abuelita visits
time seems to stop.

I begin to feel like a wise old cubana,
while she becomes young and American
as we trade our grandmother
granddaughter
two-country
stories.

Sitting side by side, we embroider
colorful stitches on circles
of soft, dream-filled cloth.

Inside my stiff embroidery hoop, a wilderness
of messy flowers starts to grow, the edges
sloppy, because needles are slippery
and my fingers feel too small
for perfection.

¡Perfecto! Abuelita says with a smile
to show that she's happy I tried.
I wait to see if she's going to follow
the island tradition of turning cloth over
to witness and judge any lumpy knots
or stray strands at the back
of a young girl's jumbled
stitches.

PAULA BARRAGÁN

"For me, drawing has become a sharp way of watching life, a powerful exploration tool that helps me invent, remember, describe, and analyze what is going on. Drawing is like using a special language with other subtleties and it is filled with nonverbal descriptions that everybody understands."

Instead, she just gives me a hug
and lets me speak of modern things
that make me sound wise
in a youthful
new-country
way.

When Abuelita visits
all the way from Cuba
both of us stroll
through gardens
of distance
embroidered
by time.

Abuelita (ah-bweh-LEE-tah): Grandma
cubana (coo-BAH-nah): Cuban; female person from Cuba
la visita (lah vee-SEE-tah): the visit
perfecto (pehr-FEHC-toh): perfect

NEIL WALDMAN

"From my earliest years, I sensed that somehow, taking a piece of white paper, and filling it with glorious colors, was an act of magic."

DOUGLAS FLORIAN

"To define poetry is like defining love:
   A poem is a glimpse.
   A poem is glimmer.
   Something that makes your whole soul shimmer.
   A poem is a taste.
   A poem is a sip.
   Something to make your whole heart flip."

Grandpa

My grandpa was a *sofer.*
A scribe of Torah scrolls.
With quill and ink on parchment
He finished rolls and rolls.
From right to left the Hebrew flowed
Without a single flaw.
And though Grandpa no longer lives
His work leaves us in awe.

sofer (SOH-fer *or* saw-FER): specially trained Jewish person who copies
   Torah scrolls
Torah (TOR-uh *or* TOH-ruh): scroll on which the first five books of the
   Bible are written

CYNTHIA LEITICH SMITH

"Poetry echoes the grandparents, sparks the fresh day."

Amazing Auntie Anne

"Huge news!
Great Auntie Anne is coming!"

I knew her through Story, only Story.
Grew up at the Indian School, back in dust-bowl days.
Took blame, punishment to spare other children.
Planned to escape.
Stayed because baby brother was too little to run.

She's all everybody can talk about.
"A millionaire!"
"Flat broke."
"College girl, nurse."
"Owns a grocery store."
"A chain of grocery stores!"
"No, an air-conditioning company."
"Speaks English. Mvskoke."
"Spanish too!"
"Spied for the US during the big war."
"A spy!"
"In Mexico!"

Mexico?

Today's the day!
Jello salad, pork, and blue dumplings,
broccoli-cheese-rice casserole.
Auntie arrives!
Waving out her window, blaring the Cadillac horn.

JEANNE ROREX BRIDGES

"The combination of my upbringing, my racial heritage, my environment, and my undeniable need to express my ideas and feelings to others is why I paint. I love to paint. I love how I feel when I paint. I thank God every day I get to live the life I live, to have this imagination and ability to paint my thoughts, my feelings, and my ideas."

"My baby brother's baby!" she exclaims.
Girl-hero, wartime-nurse, maybe-spy-millionaire.
Thrilled to meet me. Me!
She's known me through Story, only Story.
As I've known Great Auntie Anne through Story.

Until now.

Now.

As we'll meet through true Story.

blue dumpling (bloo duhm-pling): dumpling made with blue cornmeal,
    often served with corn and meat stew
Mvskoke (MA-skó-k-î): the traditional language of the Muscogee
    (Creek) Nation

NAOMI SHIHAB NYE

"Poetry is the melodious, international language that carries our minds, our hearts into deeper places than the shallow waters we splash around in all day long. For me, poetry has always been a place of great and necessary refreshment. It is the true rest stop in life. 'Pause here,' it says. 'Be filled with seeing. Say something simple and true.'"

Far, Far Away
(for Palestine)

How lonely the word *PEACE* is becoming.
She misses her small house under the olive trees.

The word *PEACE* was my daddy's ticket on the ship
to the New World. Maybe it would be his ticket back too.
He never threw it away. When I was born,
I felt a peaceful breeze waving in the branches.
Her voice pressed me forward. She told me to speak.
Our parents who did not look like one another at all
raised us in a house of stories with garlic.
Everything began, *Far, far away*. But everything held us close.

Is this your story, or mine?

We grew up near the invisible line in Ferguson that separated
white and black people. We were olive-colored people
with a white mom and very funny dad.
It seemed wrong that we could go anywhere and others
felt scared. A huge moon hummed lullabies at night.

What happens to Peace when people fight?
(She hides her face.)
What does she dream of?
(Better people.)
Does she ever give up?
(Never.)

But sometimes she feels very lonely on the earth.
She wants to walk with children.
She wants to have a party with small china cups.
Small cookies on small plates. Lots of them.
She wants everyone to share.

Ferguson (FUR-guh-suhn): city in eastern Missouri, near St. Louis

SAWSAN CHALABI

"Art is a powerful tool. One look and the viewer is transported into another's experience, feeling the emotions, understanding the thoughts, and seeing the vision of another, creating a quiet, real, and intimate connection."

RAFAEL LÓPEZ

"Painting is the voice that helps me share all those experiences and feelings that are hard to tell with words."

JORGE TETL ARGUETA

"Poetry is the opportunity to keep on dreaming, to create a colorful reality of beauty where everything is possible with words—even a just world. I believe in the magical power of words. I believe that poetry can make us dance, sing, fly, make the impossible possible—and like a sunrise, make us rise every morning and keep on dreaming."

Tepechapa River

The river of my hometown Witzapan
Is called Tepechapa

Its huge stones are faces
Of grandmothers and faces of grandfathers

The Tepechapa River sings
The Tepechapa River dreams

When you bathe in the Tepechapa
Ask for a wish to the water, said my grandmother

I don't remember what I asked for

But every time I drink water I remember
My grandmother, my people

I can fly

I can sing

I can dream

Like the Tepechapa River.

Tepechapa (teh-peh-CHAH-peh): river in El Salvador
Witzapan (WIT-zah-pan): Nawat name for a municipality in northwestern
El Salvador; Nawat (NAH-what) is a local language of El Salvador

R. GREGORY CHRISTIE

"Growing up as an aspiring artist, I spent most of my free time drawing and painting. In no time they became my preferred form of communication. Creating art for a children's book is a powerful thing because more than likely the illustrations are the first images a young person will see."

MARILYN NELSON

"What is poetry? To me poetry is shaped language."

Route 66

Daddy's been transferred, so we're in the car
moving from base to base to protect our country.
I'm in the backseat on the driver's side,
watching the landscape slide from beauty to beauty.
Sometimes I watch Daddy navigate the road,
sometimes I make up stories about cars that pass
going in a huge hurry the other way.
Is someone somewhere waiting for them to arrive?
Are they driving to something good, or from something bad?
Are they moving, as we are, to a new home?
What are the kids in their backseats dreaming?
We hum with the radio in our Kaiser.
Sometimes Mama or Daddy bursts into song.
We play word games and singing games and laugh.
I sit behind Daddy's beautiful close-shorn head
and his broad, strong uniform-blue shoulders,
loving him, and feeling fear for his life.
What if somebody who hates black people
drives past our car and shoots him in the head?

Kaiser (KAHY-zer): brand of car manufactured in the United States from
   1945 to 1953
Route 66 (root *or* rout SIKS-tee-siks): one of the original highways in
   the US Highway System, running 2,448 miles (3,940 kilometers)
   and connecting Chicago, Illinois, with Santa Monica, California;
   established in 1926 and decommissioned in 1985

NICK BRUEL

"The last time I tried to write a serious poem was in college. When the opportunity came for me to write 'Pick One' for this volume, to discuss what it was like for me to grow up defining myself as sometimes white and sometimes Chinese and sometimes both, I embraced it. Will I ever write poetry again? Almost certainly. I feel I have surmounted a bit of a hurdle."

Pick One

All I had to do was mark one box on the form.
        Just one. That's it.
        But only one.

So I asked my mother, and we walked to Chinatown
        where we ate bright yellow egg custards
        and roast pork buns
        and lao po bing, flaky outside and sweetened
            with winter melon inside.

I was just about to check the box marked
        Asian
        when I paused and said, "But I'm Chinese."
"Close enough," my mother told me.

I then asked my father, and we walked to the grocery store
        to buy potatoes for pommes frites
        and garlic butter and mussels
        and apfelstrudel, flaky outside and sweetened
            with apples inside.

I was just about to check the box marked
        Caucasian
        when I paused and said, "But I'm Belgian."
"Close enough," my father told me.

Asian. Caucasian. Pick one.

JANINE MACBETH

"Art is a superpower, a storyteller that can shed light on characters in new ways. For me, art has always been a way to honor people who are undervalued and made invisible—a way to shout our dignity and beauty."

I asked my mother again, and she reminded me
of my ancestors in the Han Dynasty who built ships
        with wood and hemp
of my great grandmother who played mahjongg
        with Madame Chiang Kai-shek
of my grandfather, a founding member of the Kuomintang.

I asked my father again, and he reminded me
of my Huguenot ancestors who scattered
        across the seas from France
of my uncle who played poker every Thursday night
        with Abbott and Costello
of my grandmother who met with Queen Victoria
        because they were cousins.

Asian. Caucasian. Pick one.

Then Mom told me about the Japanese soldier,
        the one who threw her to the ground as a child
        and upended a trash can on top of her
        shocked, sobbing body,
        covering her face in rot and debris
        and told her to be quiet or die
        moments before an army of his compatriots
        stormed the street
        and murdered hundreds.
He saved her life, this soldier.

And Dad told me of the old man,
        the one he met in the library as a child
        living in Antwerp
        who told him there was a storm coming,
        a hurricane of brown shirts and black boots
        and furious disdain for innocence
        and that he should run,
        he should find his mother and his sister and run
        to America.
He saved his life, this old man.

Asian. Caucasian. Pick one.

I chose "Other."

And below I wrote
       I am the child of two who ran
       as fast as they could
       away from the horror and the cruelty
and the madness of armies,
who ran blindly into a world they knew little about
and didn't stop running until
they happened to meet
each other.

Abbott and Costello (AB-uht and ko-STEL-oh): popular comedy team in
    the 1940s and 1950s
Antwerp (AN-twerp): seaport city in northern Belgium
apfelstrudel (ap-FELL STROO-dul): traditional Viennese layered pastry
    with apple filling
Han Dynasty (hahn DAHY-nuh-stee): second great imperial dynasty in
    China (206 BCE to 220 CE)
Huguenot (HYOO-guh-not): French Protestant of the sixteenth and
    seventeenth centuries
Kuomintang (gwoh-min-dang): political party in the Republic of China
    (Taiwan)
lao po bing (lao poh bing): traditional Cantonese Chinese pastry with thin,
    flaky crust and sweet filling
Madame Chiang Kai-shek (muh-DAM or MAD-uhm jiang kahy-SHECK):
    first lady of the Republic of China (Taiwan) from 1949 to 1975
mahjongg (mah-zhong): Chinese game played by four people using
    domino-like tiles
pommes frites (pohm freet): fried potatoes; French fries
Queen Victoria (kween vik-TOHR-ee-uh): queen of the United Kingdom of
    Great Britain and Ireland from 1837 to 1901

G. NERI

"Poetry is like dreaming through time—a visceral punch to the gut that brings everything back home again. Poetry makes the past immediate, lets you taste sea air, feel gravel on the ground, smell your grandma's cooking like you're standing right outside her window. You want to close your eyes and just breathe it in."

Gumbo Nation

Mami always done said:
when you missin' home,
make you some gumbo!

Gumbo is life—
spicy an' hot 'nuff
to make you sweat.

Gumbo is life—
rich an' brown
an' smellin' of heavenly
d'light.

Gumbo is you an' me
an' this in here
(pointing to my heart).

So stop your mopin', child!
You homesick?
Make you some gumbo
an' you'll be right at home,
no matter where you are!

Get that roux goin'!
White flour an' butter
over a hot fire
'til it turn muddy brown,
just like the M'ssippi.
The river will take you home.

CHARLOTTE RILEY-WEBB

"In my work, I find myself shifting back and forth between realism and abstraction. Realism in art is like music with lyrics. Abstraction is more like jazz and improvisation. There is a place in my artistic world for both; the rhythms and the music in my head are the same."

Then come the earth
which cradles the river—
carrot an' celery,
pepper an' onion an' tomato,
an' don't forget the okra—
soft 'nuff to slide down your throat.
Spice it up just right
till it lights up the room.
Then come the meat—
the breath of life.
You got your chicken,
your andouille sausage,
your shrimp an' crawdad.
Plus a secret flavor from your childhood—
Spam, the meat in a can!
It's the surprise ingredient (like you).
Top all that with some filé
ground from leaves of a sassafras tree,
smellin' like the sweet bayou,
deep an' full of mystery.

Gumbo is the food of your people—
African, French, Spanish, Choctaw—
stirred all together in a Creole mix
and simmered over time
under a hot Louisiana sun.
All this is part of America
an' part of you,
no matter where you are
or who you with.

You could be in California
or Florida or Minnesota
for that matter.
Get some gumbo in you,
and *CooWee!*
you'll be right home again.

So spin some rousin' zydeco tunes
an' open all the windows—
Gumbo is bein' served
an' things is about to get hot
up in here!

bayou (BAHY-oo *or* BAHY-oh): marshy or slowly flowing body of water
    filled with plants
filé (FEE-lay): powder made from the dried leaves of a sassafras tree
gumbo (GUHM-boh): thick stew or soup made with meat, seafood,
    and vegetables
Mami (MAH-mee): Mom
roux (roo): cooked mixture of flour and butter used to thicken stews
    and soups
zydeco (ZAHY-di-koh): lively blues-influenced music popular in Louisiana

JANE YOLEN

"I think of poetry as the soul of literature. It is what we see and hear the moment before sleep takes us. It is the space between wingbeats. The pause between heartbeats. The first touch of the drumstick on the tight stretch of drum hide and the slight burring after. It is also a single great line. A word discovered after an afternoon of trying. An emotion caught in the hand, in the mouth. Two words that bump up against each other and create something new. A song between friends."

Calling Home

I remember now the sycamore summers,
one long block from the bay,
how we teased the neighbor's bulldog
till he chased us teeth and tail,
both ends grinding away,
to the one big tree with the low limb
that everyone could climb but me.

I remember the mothers leaning out
into the soft southern night,
calling us home, our names
an accident of place:
Frances Bird,
Willard A. Bubba,
Mary Alice,
and me,
the northern intruder,
Jane.

How quickly the agony of August
ended all our games,
till now—in the hot, flashing winter
that is my life, I wait
beneath that phantom limb,
still awkwardly out of reach.
Behind me I hear the grinding sounds
of Miz B's bulldog. And somewhere yet

JULIE DOWNING

"I always see stories first. Whenever I read text, the first thing I imagine is a visual picture of the words. The hardest part of the process is getting my initial visual ideas down on paper. I always want the words to tell part of the story and the picture to expand the idea."

my mother leaning out of the screen door,
floral apron dusted with flour,
saying my name into the darkling dusk
and calling me—so late—back home.

JOSEPH BRUCHAC

"It is commonly said among Native Americans that the first music the child hears is the heartbeat of the mother. It is our first poetry—our first song. Poetry is powerful language; a poem is a shape that stays. Every country, every language, every culture has poetry. Poetry seems to be one of those things that human beings do, a creative urge found throughout the ages. Poems were being written thousands of years ago and many of those ancient poems are still being read today."

Rez Road

The place we live isn't very big
compared to all that once was ours.
This reservation we call home
is ten miles long and six miles wide.
But even though it's not that large,
a nice new state superhighway
cuts through the middle of maple forest—
hunting grounds where we found medicine plants.

My Grandpa Bigtree has always had
what our people call a really well
developed Indian sense of humor.
He says it all worked out for the best.
It's made hunting a whole lot easier
for us, although it now takes two—
one to stop traffic and one to run
out into the road to pick up game.
Although I know he's only kidding,
he's shown me how, if you know how to look,
you really can find our old healing plants
growing next to that four-lane road.

Sometimes tourists stray off the interstate
down onto Frog Street, where our Indian school,
box lacrosse rink, and meeting house
all crowd together with churches
and trailers and well-worn houses

in need of paint, some with cars
without wheels up on concrete blocks
parked like lawn ornaments in their front yards.

No one ever gets rich when they stay here.
Living on the rez, you learn how to share.
Tourists just don't see the things we see.
They're looking for tipis and chiefs in war bonnets,
not some dark-haired kid wearing sneakers
and headphones, bobbing his head to Indian rap.

Yeah, things seem different
than they did long ago.
Some of our own people
don't even know how
to speak our language,
though we teach it in our school.
Some hit the road and don't come back.
But some of us, like Grandpa Bigtree,
know that hidden roots still give you strength.

There will always be another day.
Four winds will always remember our names.
No matter how many roads they build,
Mother Earth is always beneath our feet.

box lacrosse (box lah-CROSS): indoor version of lacrosse; lacrosse is a contact
    sport played by two teams using a small rubber ball and long-handled sticks
rez (rez): short form of *reservation*, as in Native American Indian reservation

DAVID KANIETAKERON FADDEN

"Art for me is an ancient form of communication that elicits emotion and a reaction from the viewer. Painting is almost a spiritual process from the moment I pick up a brush and start applying pigment to canvas to when I sign it. While writers have a gift of creating stories with the pen, I feel I can tell my stories with the brush."

DANIEL MINTER

"As an artist I create images that represent a story fragment and I try to find a way to connect those individual pieces into narratives, just as we all have our personal stories that feel unique, yet there are numerous ways we are similar and connected. We need one another if we want to understand the larger story."

CAROLE BOSTON WEATHERFORD

"I aim to mine the past for family stories, forgotten struggles, and fading traditions. The Creator called me to be a poet. I hear words strung together in my head just as a composer hears notes and chords. The best poetry makes music with words."

What My Kinfolk Made

My great-great grandfathers Isaac and Phillip
who were born into slavery, made history,
founding communities after the Civil War.
My great grandmother Mary wove corn husk saddles
that she sold to save money for a small farm.
My great grandfather James built a house and barn on that land.
My great grandmother Margie was a nurse-midwife
who concocted remedies from herbs and roots
and welcomed brown babies into the world.
Her husband Lun made hot tamales and homebrew
that he sold to send two sons and a daughter to college.
One son, my grandfather, a preacher, penned Sunday sermons.
My grandmothers, Ann and Susan, baked bread
and sweets and pieced together crazy quilts
as they watched soap operas on TV.
My mother sewed dresses, curtains, and slipcovers.
My father set type, printed ephemera, tooled leather,
did decorative metalwork, built furniture, sheds,
and gazebos, and planted flower and vegetable gardens
and an orchard that still bears fruit.
How could I not strive to fashion garments from remnants,
to refinish heirloom furniture found in the barn,
to string words together into lines of verse?

How could I not strive to make something of myself?

ephemera (ih-FEM-er-uh): items originally meant to be useful for only a
short period of time, such as coupons and theater programs
midwife (MID-whyfe): person trained to help women in childbirth

JULIET MENÉNDEZ

"Nobody should feel like an outsider when they look at art, go to galleries, and read books. Each time I illustrate, I look for a new face to bring into the group of insiders."

GUADALUPE GARCÍA McCALL

"Poetry is life. It is the air we breathe, the food we eat, the songs we sing. Poetry is sunshine kissing the freckles of your cheeks, droplets of rain quivering on a leaf, snow melting in the palms of your hands, hot sand burning the soles of your feet. Poetry is laughter. Poetry is a sigh. Poetry is tears. Poetry is Everything."

My Quinceañera

Before my quinceañera, my parents took me aside.
They told me to wish, to dream. They gave me advice.
They were very loving. They were very sweet.
But I had reservations. I was getting cold feet.

What if I trip? What if I stumble and fall?
Would you think less of me if I crawled back home?

Today is special. Today you're fifteen.
We are proud of you. Today you are our Queen!
You're wearing a gown; you're sporting a bow.
This is your night. Go! Have a ball!
Listen to the music, listen to your heart.
This is your party, share your vision—make art.
Don't be afraid to dance, to twist, to twirl.
You have every right to move about in this world.

What if they hate me? I asked my father.
What if they despise me because of my color?

Some will be mean and call you *Mexican*!
Some will show prejudice; some will be sexists.
You'll want to cry. You'll want to wail.
But you can't let them stop you. You must prevail.
Some will snicker when they hear you speak.
Remember, their disrespect you can't concede.
Yes, you're different. Yes, you're brown.
But you're a Señorita—you wear a crown.

What if they laugh when I bow and curtsy?
¡Ay, papi! ¡Ay, mami! What if they reject me?

Some will be critical and stand in your way.
They'll tear you down, try to lead you astray.
But you are not weak. You know how to speak.
You're a light source, a sunbeam—you are incandescent!
Don't be so scared—from a girl, you've transcended.
As Señorita, you're to be commended.
Listen to the wind and trust in your stars.
Our ancestors were gente buena; that's who you are.

What if they question my values, my morals?
¡Ay, papi! ¡Ay, mami! I don't want to quarrel.

This Bible is part of an ancient tradition.
It's not a weapon. It's full of wisdom.
Life's not all right, but it's not all wrong.
This book of prayers will help keep you strong.
You're not stuck up. You're not discourteous.
You are Señorita. You're full of courage.
This great big world comes with joys and sorrows.
But we're your familia. We were here yesterday.
We'll be here tomorrow.

ay (eye): oh
familia (fah-MEEL-yah): family
gente buena (HEN-teh BWEH-nah): good people
mami (MAH-mee): mom, mommy
papi (PAH-pee): dad, daddy
quinceañera (keen-seen-NYEH-rrah): girl's fifteenth birthday celebration
señorita (seh-nyoh-REE-tah): young lady

ABOUT THE POETS AND ARTISTS

JACKET

Sean Qualls was born in Florida, raised in New Jersey, and currently lives in Brooklyn, New York. He has been illustrating books for young people since the early 2000s and quickly became known for his unique collage style. The projects he works on often explore

Sean, age 6

historical subjects, with an emphasis on the important issues of identity and race. Among the honors Sean's works have received are a Coretta Scott King Illustrator Award Honor, an American Library Association Notable Children's Books selection, and a Bank Street Best Children's Book of the Year. You can view a collection of his books and fine art paintings and collages on his website at seanqualls.com.

Janet, age 7

"MOTHER'S DAY" and "SPEAK UP"

Janet S. Wong was born in Los Angeles, California. After graduating from Yale University Law School, she practiced labor law at Universal Studios in Los Angeles. Her career took a dynamic turn in 1994 when her first book of poetry for children, *Good Luck Gold*, was published. Since then she has written more than two dozen award-winning books for young readers. Because of her diverse background growing up with her Chinese immigrant father and Korean immigrant mother, much of Janet's writing provides insights into the varied types of challenges and prejudices many children confront today. She lives in New Jersey, and her website is janetwong.com.

"MOTHER'S DAY"

Simone Shin, born and raised in the San Francisco Bay area of California, is an award-winning fine artist and illustrator. As the child of South Korean parents, Simone was drawn to Korean folk art, which has played a big role in the development of her artistic

Simone, age 5

style. After graduating from the ArtCenter College of Design in Pasadena, Simone worked in editorial illustration and art education, and her artwork has won a Gold Medal for Uncommissioned work from the Society of Illustrators in New York. She has also illustrated several popular picture books with images inspired by her interests in folk art, family history, music, and nature. Simone still lives in the San Francisco Bay area. Her website is simoneshin.com.

Vana Kim

Insoo, age 3

"SPEAK UP"

Insoo Kim was born in Los Angeles, California, to Korean immigrant parents. He has lived in several places around the United States as well as in South Korea, Japan, Australia, and Canada. After a year at the Rhode Island School of Design, he transferred to the Tisch School of the Arts at New York University and graduated with a bachelor of fine arts degree in film and television. Growing up, Insoo often felt on the periphery of American culture, and this has motivated him to create personal projects as well as stories about Korean history, family, and culture. He currently works as an art director, a concept artist, an illustrator, and an animator in the Los Angeles area. His website is insookimyo.com.

"HERE'S WHAT I REMEMBER"

Kwame Alexander was born in New York City to a family of artists. In addition to writing more than twenty-eight books for young readers, he is cofounder of LEAP for Ghana, an international literacy project that builds libraries, trains teachers, and

Portia Wiggins

Kwame, age 8

empowers children through literature. In 2015, Kwame received the Newbery Medal for his middle-grade verse novel *The Crossover*. He has also been honored with the Lee Bennett Hopkins Poetry Award, three NAACP Image Award nominations, and many other awards. Kwame is a regular contributor to NPR's *Morning Edition* radio broadcast and is the founder of Versify, an imprint of Houghton Mifflin Harcourt that publishes diverse books for young people of all ages. He currently lives in Virginia. His website is kwamealexander.com.

Kevin Parker

Michele, age 8 or 9

Michele Wood was born in Indianapolis, Indiana. She works as a children's book illustrator, fine artist, designer, and filmmaker. Recently she received her master of divinity degree at Christian Theological Seminary, where she was the Artist in Residence from 2015 to 2018. Michele won the Coretta Scott King Illustrator Award in 1999 for her illustrations in *i see the rhythm* and received an NAACP Image Award nomination for *Chasing Freedom* in 2016. "I want every child to have exposure to books that reflect their experiences," Michele says. "Every young mind can succeed with exposure to books that reflect and engage." She lives in Florida, and her website is michelewood.com.

"LA VISITA"

Margarita Engle was born and raised in Los Angeles, California. After seeing photographs of Cuba in *National Geographic*, her father traveled to the island. There he met Margarita's mother and they married. Margarita's childhood summers were spent

Margarita, age 7

in Cuba, where she developed deep family bonds and later found the inspiration for many of her books. Her works have won numerous awards and honors. In 2009, she became the first Latinx to receive a Newbery Medal Honor for her verse novel *The Surrender Tree*, and she has been honored six times by the Pura Belpré Author Award. Margarita also served as the 2017–19 national Young People's Poet Laureate. She lives in central California and her website is margaritaengle.com.

Paula, age 4

Paula Barragán was born in Quito, Ecuador, and studied graphic design and illustration at Pratt Institute in New York. She creates in various media, including painting, engraving, and drawing; and her work has been shown in many international galleries and exhibitions.

For more than three decades, Paula has operated her own workshop in Quito, where she still lives. She designs logos, posters, illustrations, art books, book covers, carpets, and more. Paula's lively, colorful, graphic illustrations draw inspiration from her Latin American roots and began appearing in picture books in 2001 with the publication of *Love to Mamá*, a collection of poetry celebrating mothers. Her website is paulabarragan.com.

"GRANDPA"

Douglas Florian, poet and artist, was born, raised, and currently lives in New York City. His father was also an artist. He encouraged Douglas to paint and suggested he enroll in an art course at the School of Visual Arts when he was fifteen years old. Douglas was

Douglas, age 4

inspired to try writing poetry after finding a book of poems, *Oh, That's Ridiculous*, edited by William Cole, at a flea market. Douglas's numerous acclaimed children's books are known for their creative poems, which often include rhyme, wordplay, emotion, and/or humor to engage readers. He is a past winner of the Lee Bennett Hopkins Poetry Award and the Claudia Lewis Poetry Award. His work is online at floriancafe.blogspot.com.

Neil, age 7

Neil Waldman was born in Bronx, New York. As a child he loved to draw and create images of what lived in his imagination. Early in his career Neil won a gold medal from the United Nations for his poster representing the International Year of Peace (1986). In addition to his work as a fine artist, he has illustrated more than fifty books for young readers, including several that he also wrote. His books have won the Christopher Award and the National Jewish Book Award, among many other honors. In 2006, Neil founded the Fred Dolan Art Academy to provide art instruction to Bronx students while guiding them to build professional portfolios. He lives in White Plains, New York, and his website is artsnet.net/waldman/.

"AMAZING AUNTIE ANNE"

Cynthia Leitich Smith, a citizen of the Muscogee (Creek) Nation, was born in Kansas City, Missouri, and lived in several states before settling in Austin, Texas, where she currently lives. After graduating from the University of Kansas, she enrolled

Cynthia, age 6

at the University of Michigan Law School, intending to become a legal journalist. During a law clerkship, Cynthia realized that her calling was elsewhere, and she began writing for children—first picture books and then speculative and realistic fiction for young adults. Her books often focus on the lives of modern-day Native American characters. A *New York Times* bestselling author, Cynthia also writes poetry, short stories, and nonfiction essays. Her website is cynthialeitichsmith.com.

Jeanne, age 7

Jeanne Rorex Bridges was born and grew up in Oktaha, Oklahoma. She is a Native artist of Cherokee ancestry who still lives on the same family farmland where she was raised. As a child Jeanne was fascinated by the way her sculptor uncle could express feelings and thoughts through simple designs. Even then, Jeanne knew she wanted to do the same through her art. Her work today derives from the flat style of painting while adding background work and shading. She is also the illustrator of the picture book *Crossing Bok Chitto,* which received several honors, including the American Library Association Notable Children's Books list and the Texas Bluebonnet Masterlist. Her website is rorexbridgesart.com.

"FAR, FAR AWAY"

Naomi Shihab Nye, born in St. Louis, Missouri, to a Palestinian father and a German-Swiss American mother, grew up in St. Louis, Jerusalem, and San Antonio, Texas, where she now lives. While living in Jerusalem she developed a strong bond with

Naomi, age 7

her Arab community. In the United States, her experiences as an Arab American are often expressed in poems about peace and heritage, and her books of poetry and fiction for children and young adults are acclaimed for their cultural awareness and sensitivity. Naomi, the 2019–21 national Young People's Poet Laureate, believes that library shelves should have more books that acquaint children with diverse voices from around the world. More information about her can be found online at poetryfoundation.org/poets/naomi-shihab-nye.

Sawsan, age 4

Sawsan Chalabi is a Lebanese American illustrator and designer. She grew up in Lebanon and Ghana, so from childhood she was exposed to people of different backgrounds both culturally and artistically. She moved to the United States after graduating from college in Lebanon and eventually left the corporate world to pursue her passion for art and illustration, earning her MFA at the Savannah College of Art and Design. When illustrating the words of a poem, story, or article, Sawsan favors simple but strong and conceptual imagery to convey the meaning as well as the mood and spirit of the written piece. She lives in Arlington, Virginia, and her website is schalabi.com.

"TEPECHAPA RIVER"

Jorge Tetl Argueta, a Pipil Nahua Indian, was born in El Salvador, where his family owned a small restaurant. Due to political unrest in his country, he came to the United States in 1980. He is a prize-winning poet and the author of more than twenty books

Jorge, age 3

for children, many of them bilingual. In 2017, he received the Lee Bennett Hopkins Poetry Award for his book *Somos como las nubes/We Are Like the Clouds*. Jorge is also the founder of the Library of Dreams in El Salvador, a nonprofit organization that promotes literacy in both rural and metropolitan areas of El Salvador. He lives and works in San Francisco, California, and San Salvador, El Salvador.

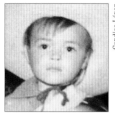

Candice López

Rafael, age 6

Rafael López was born in Mexico City and grew up in a suburb of that city. As a young boy, he connected with stories and drawing, fascinated by imagery from different lands and cultures. As an artist, he is influenced by Mexican surrealism, from which he developed his unique style. For the picture books he illustrates, Rafael creates diverse characters that reflect and honor the lives of all young people. His books have been recognized five times by the Pura Belpré Illustrator Award, among many other honors. He is also a founder of the Urban Art Trail movement in San Diego, creating community-based murals. He lives part-time in San Diego, California, and part-time in central Mexico. His website is rafaellopez.com.

"ROUTE 66"

Melvin M. Nelson Sr.

Curt Richter

Marilyn, age 4

Marilyn Nelson was born in Cleveland, Ohio. Her mother was a teacher and her father was an Air Force officer. During her youth, Marilyn lived on various military bases, often the only black child at schools she attended. Her memoir, *How I Discovered Poetry*, tells about growing up and traveling around the United States amid the racial tensions of the 1950s. Marilyn's groundbreaking young adult book, *Carver: A Life in Poems*, was awarded both a Newbery Medal Honor and a Coretta Scott King Author Award Honor. In 2017, she was the recipient of the National Council of Teachers of English (NCTE) Award for Excellence in Poetry for Children. She lives in Connecticut, and her website is marilyn-nelson.com.

Gregory, age 7 or 8

R. Gregory Christie was born and raised in New Jersey. He demonstrated a talent for art at an early age, and his first illustration was published in a newspaper while he was still in art school. Since then, Gregory has illustrated album covers, festival posters, advertisements, and more than sixty books, several of which are biographies of significant historical or cultural figures. He was awarded a Caldecott Medal Honor for his illustrations in *Freedom in Congo Square*. He is also a six-time Coretta Scott King Illustrator Award honoree. In 2012, Gregory founded GAS-ART Gifts, a bookstore and art studio where people can admire artwork and create it themselves. He lives in the Atlanta, Georgia, area. His website is gas-art.com.

"PICK ONE"

Nick, age 6

Nick Bruel was born in New York City to a Chinese mother and a Belgian father. His full name is Nicholas Tung Ming Bruel. His wife, Carina, is of Italian and French Canadian ancestry, and they have an adopted daughter from Vietnam. Nick, best known as the creator of the humorous *New York Times* bestselling Bad Kitty series, embraced the opportunity to take on the serious subject of his racial identity. "Pick One" reflects his experiences having to define his race on official documents. "I'm sometimes at a loss for how to answer since I'm not entirely Asian, I'm not entirely white, and 'Other' doesn't seem to fit at all," says Nick. He lives in Westchester County, New York, and his websites are nickbruel.com and badkittybooks.com.

Janine, age 6

Janine Macbeth was born and raised in Oakland, California, and is of Asian, Black, white, and Native ancestry. She has wanted to create children's books since she was a child, but when authors and illustrators of color were absent from the books in her school library, Janine followed her passion for racial justice instead. Years later, while working at a nonprofit organization, she founded Blood Orange Press to publish the diverse books she yearned for when she was growing up. Janine is a mostly self-taught artist who wrote and illustrated *Oh, Oh, Baby Boy!*, her first book, which was released in 2013. She still lives in Oakland today. Her websites are j9macbeth.com and bloodorangepress.com.

"GUMBO NATION"

Greg, age 4

G. Neri was raised in Los Angeles, California, then moved to Santa Cruz to attend college and pursue a career in filmmaking. He later taught animation and storytelling to inner-city teens, producing more than three hundred films. His heritage is Creole, Filipino, and Mexican, which he says is "a great example of globalization." He is the author of ten books for young readers. His debut free-verse novel, *Chess Rumble*, inspired by inner-city school chess enrichment programs, received the 2010 Lee Bennett Hopkins/International Literacy Association Promising Poet Award, and his graphic novel *Yummy: The Last Days of a Southside Shorty*, was awarded a Coretta Scott King Author Award Honor. He lives in Florida, and his website is gneri.com.

Charlotte, age 7

Charlotte Riley-Webb was born in Atlanta, Georgia, and grew up in Cleveland, Ohio. She earned her BFA degree from the Cleveland Institute of Art and continues to explore new mediums through workshops and classes. Her paintings are included in corporate, museum, and private collections as well as public art installations throughout the United States and abroad. Charlotte's signature rhythmic style, with its bright, exuberant colors and strokes, is reflected in both her abstract and representational paintings, and easily translated into the illustrations for eight picture books. Her first, *Rent Party Jazz*, was read by Oscar Award–winning actress Viola Davis for Storyline Online, the SAG-AFTRA Foundation's children's literacy program. Charlotte lives in Stockbridge, Georgia. Her website is charlotterileywebb.com.

"CALLING HOME"

Jane Yolen, born in New York City, grew up in a literary environment. Her father wrote books and scripts for radio broadcasts, and her mother created crossword puzzles that appeared in children's magazines. In 1963, just three years after graduating

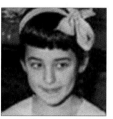

Jason Stemple
Jane, age 6

from college, Jane's first book was published. Decades later her career continues to flourish. She has written more than 375 books, including picture books, young adult novels, science fiction, fantasy, and poetry for all ages. Jane has won numerous awards for her works, and her modern classic, *Owl Moon*, has been in print for more than thirty years. She divides her time between homes in Hatfield, Massachusetts, and St. Andrews, Scotland, and her website is janeyolen.com.

Nancy Downing

Lorenz Angelo
Julie, age 4

Julie Downing was born and raised in Denver, Colorado. As a child she loved to draw and paint, but thought she would grow up to be an actor. After receiving her MFA degree from the Rhode Island School of Design, Julie turned her enjoyment of creating characters and acting out stories to painting images for picture books. Her rich, jewel-like watercolors can be seen in the more than forty-five popular books she has illustrated, and her paintings have been exhibited in galleries throughout the United States and England. In addition, Julie teaches undergraduate and graduate students at the Academy of Art University in San Francisco, California, where she also lives. Her website is juliedowning.com.

"REZ ROAD"

Joseph Bruchac was born in Saratoga Springs, New York, and grew up in Greenfield Center, New York, where he still lives. Raised by his grandparents, Joseph recalls sitting next to a potbellied stove in their general store listening to Adirondack

Joseph, age 9

tall tales, stories, and songs. He is a poet and the author of more than 130 books, many of which draw on his Abenaki ancestry. In addition to creating a wide range of titles for readers of all ages, Joseph is a storyteller and musician who performs throughout the United States and Europe. He believes "every human being shares the drumbeat of the heart and we must all share the heartbeat of the earth." His website is josephbruchac.com.

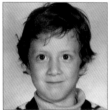
David, age 5

David Kanietakeron Fadden, Wolf Clan Mohawk, was born in Lake Placid, New York, and grew up in nearby Onchiota in a family of artists, naturalists, and storytellers. Although he did not attend art school, David learned from his father, an art teacher and illustrator; his mother, a wood sculptor and potter; and his paternal grandfather, an educator, a storyteller, and the founder of Six Nations Indian Museum. David's illustrations have appeared in books, periodicals, and animations, and on television. He also works as a cultural interpreter at the Native North American Travelling College and helps run his grandfather's museum during the busy summer months. David lives in Akwesasne, Ontario, Canada. His artwork is online at sixnationsindianmuseum.com/art.html.

"WHAT MY KINFOLK MADE"

Carole Boston Weatherford, born and raised in Baltimore, Maryland, was in first grade when she dictated her first poem to her mother. The poem alerted her parents to her gift. A driving force in all her writing is to "mine the past for family stories,

Carole, age 9

fading traditions, and forgotten struggles." Carole's first book for children appeared in 1995. Since then she has written dozens more books, most of them in verse, that explore African American lives and events. Her works have received numerous awards, including Coretta Scott King Award Honors and NAACP Image Awards. She is also a recipient of the Lee Bennett Hopkins Poetry Award. Carole lives in North Carolina. Her website is cbweatherford.com.

Daniel Minter was born in Ellaville, Georgia. As a child he liked to spend time outside and in the woods, listening to and observing his surroundings. Today his ideas for his artwork still come from observing the natural world, as well as from social interactions with people and thinking about

Daniel, age 7 or 8

history and science. Daniel has illustrated more than ten picture books and has received a Coretta Scott King Illustrator Award Honor for his images in *Ellen's Broom*. He is a founder of the Indigo Arts Alliance and the founding director of Maine Freedom Trails, an organization dedicated to identifying sites related to the history of African Americans in Maine. Daniel lives in Portland, Maine, and his website is danielminter.net.

Guadalupe, age 6

"MY QUINCEAÑERA"

Guadalupe García McCall was born in Piedras Negras, Coahula, Mexico, and at age six moved with her family to the United States, where she grew up in Eagle Pass, Texas. Over the years she kept close ties with relatives on both sides of the US-Mexico border, and when she began to write, Eagle Pass or Piedras Negras became the setting for her novels and most of her poems. For her first book, the verse novel *Under the Mesquite*, Guadalupe won the Pura Belpré Author Award, the Lee Bennett Hopkins / International Literacy Association Promising Poet Award, and several other honors. She is an assistant professor of English at George Fox University and lives in the Pacific Northwest. Her website is guadalupegarciamccall.com.

Juliet Menéndez was born in the United States to a Guatemalan father and an Irish American mother. She grew up in the Washington, DC, area and Guatemala City amid many traditions that reflected both her parents' heritages. She studied art in the United States and Italy, and design in

Juliet, age 3

France, all of which led her to develop her distinctive flat, graphic illustration style. Coming from a bicultural family and as a former bilingual teacher in New York City, Juliet sees the need for more books that depict children from diverse backgrounds and that include varied perspectives and characters. She divides her time among Guatemala City, New York City, and Paris. Her website is julietmenendez.com.